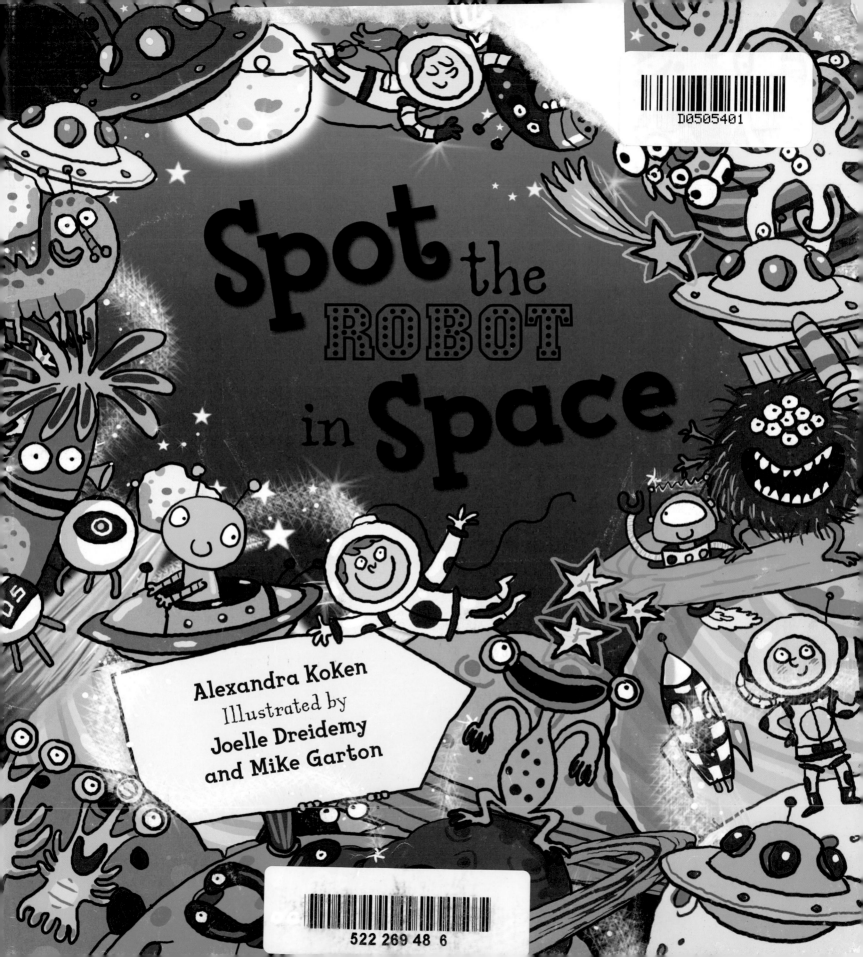

Spot the ROBOT in Space

Alexandra Koken

Illustrated by
Joelle Dreidemy
and Mike Garton

Welcome to space!

There's lots to see. Come and have a look!

Earth

Mars

Our Solar System

Planet Zorgoop!

This robot is hiding inside the book. Can you find him in every scene?

Because there is no gravity in space, everything floats!

Our Solar System includes the Sun and eight planets that orbit around it.

Uranus

Sun

Jupiter

Neptune

Earth

It looks as though there's life on this planet! Which alien is the smallest?

Can you spot these things?

asteroid   button   butterfly   controls   spaceship

Do you think aliens exist? Maybe they live in a city like this...

UFO stands for unidentified flying object.

Can you spot these things?

scarf   goggles   necklace   ear muffs   party hat

Planet Earth has the only life we know of... so far!

Can you spot these things?

octopus   flag   ship

Eiffel Tower   bird

More to spot

Go back and find these scenes in the book!

Did you find me?

Did you Know?

Valentina Tereshkova was the first woman in space in 1963. She was 26 years old.

One of the first animals in space was a Russian dog called Laika.

We can see some planets in the night sky because they reflect light from the Sun.

To take off, a rocket needs power to escape Earth's gravity. It burns gas to push away from Earth.

In 1938, a story based on a science fiction book called *War of the Worlds* was performed on the radio. Thousands of listeners thought that aliens were really invading Earth!

More space fun!

Life in space

Imagine what it would be like if people lived on another planet. Draw your ideas! Would there be flying cars? What would the houses look like? Would pets have to wear space suits?

Make your own robot

Using empty kitchen rolls, small boxes and tin foil; make your own robot. Use sticky tape to join all the parts together, and then cover them in the foil for a robot-look. You can use stickers to add buttons, controls and a face.

Hide and seek

Choose a cuddly toy to hide around your home for a friend or family member to find, just like the robot in the book! You could hide other objects and make a list of things to find.

Alien shapes

Cut out pictures of people, animals, machines and plants from a magazine. Remember to ask an adult for permission. Cut each of your pictures into bits and mix them up. Put them back together but in new combinations. For example, a man's head with a dog's body on bicycle wheels!

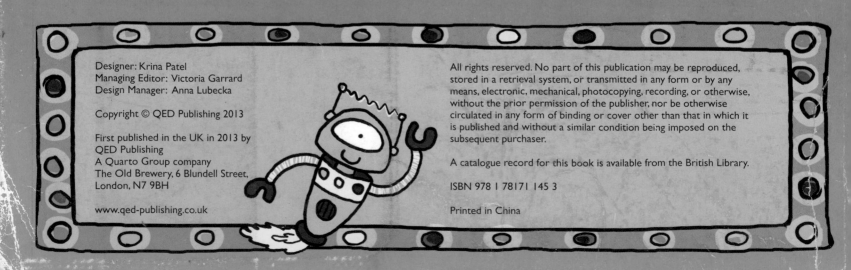

Designer: Krina Patel
Managing Editor: Victoria Garrard
Design Manager: Anna Lubecka

Copyright © QED Publishing 2013

First published in the UK in 2013 by
QED Publishing
A Quarto Group company
The Old Brewery, 6 Blundell Street,
London, N7 9BH

www.qed-publishing.co.uk

A catalogue record for this book is available from the British Library.

ISBN 978 1 78171 145 3

Printed in China